SPIRIT OF

NARROW GAUGE STEAM

ROBIN JONES

To Jenny, Vicky and Ross

First published in Great Britain in 2011

British Library Cataloguing-in-Publication Data
A CIP record for this title is available from the British Library

ISBN 978 0 85710 050 4

PiXZ Books
Halsgrove House, Ryelands Business Park,
Bagley Road, Wellington, Somerset TA21 9PZ
Tel: 01823 653777
Fax: 01823 216796
email: sales@halsgrove.com

An imprint of Halstar Ltd, part of the Halsgrove group of companies
Information on all Halsgrove titles is available at: www.halsgrove.com

Printed and bound in China by Toppan Leefung Printing Ltd

Introduction

Britain invented, through Cornish mining engineer Richard Trevithick, the railway locomotive in the form of the self-propelled steam engine, and it superseded the horse traction that had gone before. Britain also showed that the railway locomotive could handle a rich and varied range of tasks by adapting not only its design, size and power, but the type of railway on which it ran.

When today we say 'narrow gauge', we mean any railways where the rails of the tracks are spaced less than 4ft 8½ins apart. Above this, we have broad gauge.

The 4ft 8½in 'standard gauge' was chosen in the 1820s by George Stephenson, inventor of the *Rocket*, who calculated the average distance between the wheels of the axles of horse-drawn cars and mineral wagons, which would have been used on the pioneer steam-operated colliery lines in his native County Durham, the cradle of the steam railway concept. Challenged in the south and west of England by Isambard Kingdom Brunel's 7ft 0¼in gauge, nonetheless Stephenson's 4ft 8½in (referred to as 'narrow gauge' by the Victorians) eventually won the day, and became considered to be the 'standard gauge'. As such it was adopted throughout Europe and North America and many other countries as the 'normal' gauge.

Narrow gauge had, however, a much older pedigree, and played a vital part in the Industrial Revolution which laid the foundations for the steam railway concept.

The earliest recorded railway was at a mine in Bohemia in 1556, and this was 2ft gauge. In Britain, horse-drawn railways exclusively served industry, connecting mines, quarries and factories to tran-

3

shipment points on rivers and canals and at sea ports. They included the 3ft 6in Little Eaton Gangway of 1793, the 2ft gauge Llandegai Tramway of 1798, the 4ft 2in gauge Surrey Iron Railway of 1803, the world's first public railway to be incorporated, and the 4ft gauge Llanelly and Mynydd Mawr Railway, which in May 1803 became the world's first public railway to begin operations.

The Penydarren Tramroad, over which Trevithick gave the world's first public demonstration of a steam locomotive in 1804, hauling a train of wagons, was 4ft gauge. In 1808 Trevithick gave public rides on a circular track near the present site of Euston Station behind another locomotive, called *Catch Me Who Can*. It therefore became the world's first steam-hauled passenger train, although the gauge is not known.

In 1812, the 4ft 1in gauge Middleton Railway in Leeds became the first in the world to make commercial use of steam traction, but solely for freight haulage.

After the success of *Rocket* at the Rainhill Trials of 1829 established steam locomotive technology as the future for public transport, a network of inter-city railways covered Britain within two decades.

At first, there were those who considered that using steam locomotive on anything less than standard gauge would compromise safety, particularly if passenger trains were being pulled.

When the 13½-mile Festiniog Railway was built between 1833-36 to 1ft 11½in gauge, linking the slate quarries of Blaenau Ffestiniog to Porthmadog Harbour, it relied on horse and gravity traction: the horse pulled the empty wagons up the continuous incline from the harbour, while the loaded wagons ran down under their own weight, controlled by a brakeman operating a lever on the front wagon.

The Festiniog Railway 'upgraded' to steam haulage in 1863, although the nearby Padarn Railway had done so in 1848. Perhaps more importantly, the Festiniog introduced steam-hauled passenger services in 1865. In doing so it became the world's first steam-operated railway providing both freight and passenger services on such a small gauge and it laid the foundations for the introduction of locomotive-worked narrow gauge railways throughout the world. Another major British first!

Just as the development of the coal, iron and steel industries in County Durham and Teesside paved the way for the development of the steam locomotive, so the slate industry of North Wales nurtured the narrow gauge version. The narrow glaciated valleys and steep mountainsides meant that narrow gauge railways offered greater versatility on difficult terrain and proved far more cost effective than standard gauge could ever hope to be. The major mining regions of Bethesda, Llanberis, Blaenau Ffestiniog and Corris all developed a network of railways of varying gauges to serve their slate quarries. The Corris and the Talyllyn chose the very unusual 2ft 3in gauge, while the Padarn Railway went for 4ft gauge.

Outside Wales, other industries started to use narrow gauge railways to move freight, notably ironstone, limestone, china clay, brick clay and metals.

The Isle of Man was somewhat late in building railways, and did so largely because of the growing Victorian tourist trade. The network then was designed as a slimmed-down version of the mainland system, with 3ft gauge chosen to cut costs, and because there would of course be no direct rail connection with the rest of Britain. Ireland also opted for 3ft gauge systems such as the sprawling County Donegal Railway network.

Mainland Britain also chose narrow gauge for lines serving sparsely-populated rural communities which main line companies did not think justified a standard gauge branch on economic grounds. There was the 2ft 6in gauge Leek & Manifold Valley Light Railway and 2ft gauge Ashover Light Railway in Derbyshire, the 2ft gauge Southwold Railway in Suffolk, the 1ft 11½in gauge Lynton & Barnstaple Railway in Devon, the 2ft 6in gauge Campbeltown & Machrihanish Light Railway in

Kintyre and 2ft 6in gauge Welshpool & Llanfair Light Railway in Montgomeryshire, to name but a few.

By late Victorian times, the public fascination with steam railways had reached the point where they began to be built for pleasure and tourist purposes. The Eaton Hall Railway in Cheshire was built for the Duke of Westminster at his private Eaton Hall estate to a gauge of 1ft 3in.

In 1915, the Fairbourne Railway, a horse-drawn affair which has been used for carrying passengers to the Barmouth ferry, was converted to a 15in gauge pleasure line. Much the same happened to the longer 3ft gauge Ravenglass & Eskdale Railway in the Lake District, which also employed scaled-down versions of main line locomotives for motive power. These paved the way for the Romney, Hythe & Dymchurch Railway built by millionaire racing driver Captain JEP Howey and which, opened in 1927, for decades boasted that it was the world's smallest public railway.

The advent of cheaper road transport and mass car ownership halted the expansion of the British railway network in the 20th century, and many classic narrow gauge lines either lost their passenger services or were closed altogether in the 1930s.

However, the takeover of the near-defunct Talyllyn Railway by a team of volunteers under the late transport enthusiast Tom Rolt in 1951 followed soon afterwards by the revival of the Festiniog (now Ffestiniog) Railway under the wing of Alan Pegler, the man who later bought *Flying Scotsman* from British Railways, launched today's railway preservation movement, which has grown to be a major player in the 21st century tourist market. Not only have many of the great narrow gauge lines along with their locomotives and stock been restored, but new lines have been laid along disused standard gauge trackbeds, and more revival schemes are underway.

This book looks at the finest of Britain's narrow gauge steam today.

1848 – Magnificent 0-4-0 *Fire Queen* was supplied new by marine engineers A Horlock and Co to the 4ft gauge Padarn Railway, and with long-scrapped sister *Jenny Lind*, was one of only two locomotives built by this firm. It is now a prize exhibit in the National Trust's splendid Penrhyn Castle Railway Museum. The Padarn Railway had been opened in 1840 using horse traction and became the first of the slate lines to use steam locomotives, albeit for freight only.

1863 – Festiniog Railway manager Charles Easton Spooner signed a contract with George England and Company of New Cross, Surrey, to supply four saddle tanks in 1863/64. They were the first truly successful 1ft 11½in gauge engines built commercially. Three of them, No 1 *Princess*, No 2, *Prince* (pictured opposite during the reopening of the Welsh Highland Railway route through the Aberglaslyn Pass in 2009) and No 4 *Palmerston* survive, the latter two in working order today.

1864 *(below)* – The Talyllyn Railway followed quickly in the footsteps of the Festiniog and obtained its first locomotive, Fletcher Jennings 0-4-2ST No 1 *Talyllyn*, in 1864. It is pictured at Tywyn Wharf Station on 6 October 2010, staging a 60th anniversary re-enactment of the last train run by the railway prior to preservationists taking over.

1866 – The Talyllyn ordered a second locomotive from Fletcher Jennings, an engineering company at Lowca near Whitehaven, Cumbria, an 0-4-0 well tank No 2 *Dolgoch*.

1869 – In 1869 the Festiniog Railway's first double Fairlie articulated locomotive, *Little Wonder*, was introduced, and these double-ended machines have since become an internationally-recognised trademark of today's line.

Designer Robert Francis Fairlie took the view that the conventional pattern of locomotive design was seriously deficient, because it wasted weight on unpowered wheels and on a tender that did nothing but carry fuel and water without contributing to the locomotive's adhesive weight. Also, 'normal' locomotives had a quite different front and rear, and were not intended to be driven backwards for long periods, making the regular use of turntables necessary.

Fairlie's answer was to have a double-ended locomotive, one which carried all its fuel and water aboard and have every axle driven. His locomotives would have twin boilers joined back-to-back at the firebox ends, with the smokeboxes at each end, and controls at both ends of a central cab to allow the engine to be driven equally well in either direction. Pictured is *Little Wonder*, sadly long since scrapped.

1873/1910 – Between 1873 and 1926, 15 Beyer Peacock 2-4-0Ts were delivered to the Isle of Man for use on the 3ft gauge steam-operated lines there. Several are still in service today, including No 10 *Kissack*.

1873 (*opposite*) – One of the first three locomotives supplied to the Isle of Man Railway, Beyer Peacock No 3 *Pender* is the only one to have left the island, and is now a sectioned exhibit in the Museum of Science & Industry in Manchester.

1876/1999 – For those customers who preferred a more conventional locomotive, Fairlie also produced single versions of his famous double-ended locomotives. The Festiniog owned a single Fairlie, the 1876-built 0-4-0T *Taliesin*, which was scrapped in 1935. A replica was built at Boston Lodge in 1999, but as it includes some parts from the original, some consider it a 'rebuild' rather than a copy. It is seen at Porthmadog Harbour Station.

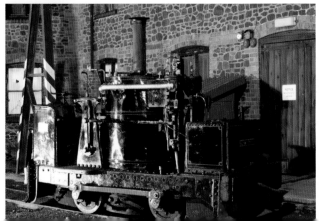

1877 – Leighton Buzzard Railway-based De Winton vertical-boilered locomotive *Chaloner*, was built for Pen-yr-Orsedd Quarry in the Nantlle valley in Caernarfonshire.

1877/2004 – Stephen Lewin & Company of Poole in Dorset, a firm much better known for building steamboats, built two diminutive locomotives for the 19in gauge Great Laxey Mines internal railway on the Isle of Man. Standing just 4ft 9in tall and 3ft wide, the pair, named *Ant* and *Bee*, could pull up to seven of the lead and zinc mine's 200 wagons each. They were too small to have cabs, and because of the low clearances in the tunnels, drivers had to remain seated. They were later scrapped, but in 2004, Great Northern Steam Ltd of Darlington, supplied full-size replicas of both to the Laxey & Lonan Heritage Trust, which reopened the railway as a tourist attraction on 25 September that year. *Bee*, with *Ant* behind, are pictured hauling three replica ore wagons.

1878 – The horse-worked 2ft 3in gauge Corris Railway in mid-Wales was acquired by a London company, Imperial Tramways Ltd, in 1878. Three steam locomotives from the Hughes Locomotive & Tramway Engine Works Ltd at Falcon Works in Loughborough (later the Brush Electrical Engineering Company) were supplied along with 10 coaches, but passenger services were not introduced for another five years due to a dispute with quarry owners. This Hughes 0-4-2ST, originally built as an 0-4-0T, became the line's No 3 and was named *Sir Haydn*.

1879 *(opposite)* – The oldest of the six Festiniog double Fairlies to survive is No 10 *Merddin Emrys*, named after the sixth century Welsh poet, was delivered in 1879 and is still in regular service today. It underwent a major rebuild in 1987/8 with new tanks. It is seen heading a vintage train along Tank Curve in deepest slate country.

1883 *(opposite)* – Former Penrhyn Quarry Hunslet 0-4-0ST *Lilian*, like so many of its sisters, found that there was certainly life after the slate industry. It was the first locomotive to run on the 1ft 11½in Launceston Steam Railway, which the locomotive's owner built on part of the standard gauge North Cornwall Railway trackbed, and which opened on Boxing Day 1983. 'Quarry Hunslets' became a generic term for the little saddle tank workhorses of the great North Wales slate mines, and 52 were built, many surviving into preservation.

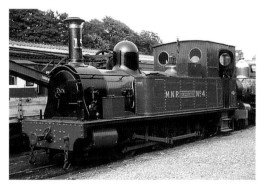

1885 – The odd man out on the Isle of Man, unique Dübs 0-6-0T *Caledonia* was supplied new to the Manx Northern Railway and in 1905 became No 15 in the Isle of Man Railway fleet, where it is still in service alongside the Beyer Peacock 2-4-0Ts which comprise the rest of the 3ft gauge line's steam fleet.

1886 – Hunslet 0-4-0ST *Velinheli* as built in 1886 for Dinorwic Quarry, was last used there on 17 September 1962. Later used on the private Inny Valley Railway in Cornwall until it closed in 1986, it afterwards moved to the Launceston Steam Railway.

1886 – A fourth double Fairlie, No 11 *Livingston Thompson*, was built at the Festiniog Railway's own Boston Lodge Works in 1886. It is now on loan to the National Railway Museum at York.

1889 – India's 2ft gauge Darjeeling Himalayan Railway has often been described as a British heritage line by the back door, for it was the British who built it between 1879 and 1881 and supplied locomotives and stock. The line rises from 328ft at Siliguri to about 7,218 ft at Darjeeling, which was developed as a sanatorium for British soldiers. In 1999, the 51-mile line was listed by UNESCO as a World Heritage Site.

Locomotive No 19 was built by Sharp Stewart of Glasgow in 1889 and after withdrawl from service in 1960, it was sold to an American enthusiast. In 2002, it was repatriated by Chiltern Railways managing director Adrian Shooter and fully restored at Tyseley Locomotive Works, Birmingham, to haul a pair of replica Darjeeling carriages built by the Ffestiniog Railway. The train runs at Adrian's private Beeches Light Railway in Oxfordshire (pictured) but visits other heritage lines.

1889, 1904, 1922 – Three ex-Dinorwic Quarry Hunslet 0-4-0STs together on the Llanberis Lake Railway in 2009: opposite, in blue is *Wild Aster* (built 1904), red *Elidir* (1889) and yellow *Dolbadarn* (1922). This modern-day 1ft 11½in gauge railway which opened in 1971 is laid on part of the 4ft gauge Padarn Railway which closed in 1961.

1891 *(below)* – Former Dinorwic Quarry Hunslet 0-4-0ST *Cloister* now hauls passenger trains at Amberley Museum in Sussex.

1893 – When the neighbouring Penrhyn Railway closed in 1962, the Ffestiniog Railway bought two of its Hunslet 2-4-0STs, *Linda* and *Blanche*, and added tenders.

1895 *(right)* – This unusual 0-4-0T, named *Spence*, was built by W Spence of Dublin for use on the internal 1ft 10in gauge system at the city's Guinness brewery. The brewer donated it to the Narrow Gauge Railway Museum at Tywyn in 1956.

1895 – The Snowdon Mountain Railway is Britain's only Swiss-style rack and pinion line, and is built to the unusual gauge of 2ft 7½in. No 2 *Enid*, an 0-4-2T named after the lady who cut the first sod, and built for the opening of the 4½-mile line up the highest mountain in Wales, passes Clogwyn.

1896 – Pictured is No 5 *Moel Siabod*, also one of the first batch of locomotives supplied by Swiss manufacturer SLM for the Snowdon line's opening in 1896. The most distinctive feature of rack railway steam locomotives is that they are built with their boilers, cab and general superstructure tilted forward at an angle. Steam engines can operate only when the boiler is level, as they require water to cover the boiler tubes and firebox sheets at all times.

1897 – *Isabel* was one of the earliest locomotives to be built to the design of EE Baguley, and delivered new by WG Bagnall of Stafford to the Cliffe Hill Granite Company of Markfield, Leicestershire, being named after one of the quarry owner's daughters. Taken out of service in 1946, it escaped the scrpaman by being repurchased by Bagnall for cosmetic restoration by apprentices. After several periods of being displayed on plinths, including a site opposite Stafford Station, the Stafford Narrow Gauge Railway Society Ltd was formed in the early 1980s to  restore it to working order. A 2ft gauge line, the Amerton Railway, at nearby Stowe-by-Chartley, was built especially for *Isabel* which ran its first revenue-earning trains there in July 1992.

1899 *(opposite)* – Running on 4ft 6in gauge track, this Peckett 0-4-0ST represents the widest narrow gauge of all. *Lee Moor No 2*, now preserved at the South Devon Railway's Buckfastleigh headquarters, was one of only two steam engines supplied to the Lee Moor Tramway, which had been laid to the local 'Dartmoor gauge' and took china clay from the Lee Moor pits to Plymouth's Sutton Harbour. Most of the tramway fell into disuse by the late forties, leaving only a short section worked by horses (and which famously crossed the GWR main line on the level) until 1960. *Lee Moor No 1* is preserved at the Wheal Martyn China Clay Museum near St Austell.

1901 – Who says railway engineering is a man's world? Kay Bowman, wife of Launceston Steam Railway founder Nigel Bowman, has restored ex-Dorothea Quarry Hunslet 0-4-0ST *Dorothea* from scrap to working order. Borrowing the boiler from sister *Covertcoat*, Kay is seen driving *Dorothea* on its maiden heritage era run in 2001. Her feat earned her the Heritage Railway Association's John Coiley Award for Locomotive Restoration.

1902 *(opposite)* – Beyer Peacock supplied two 0-6-0Ts for the 1903 opening of the 2ft 6in gauge Welshpool & Llanfair Light Railway, one of the few narrow gauge branch lines to be built under the 1896 Light Railways Act. Both passed into preservation along with the line. A Centenary Special working on 5 April 2003 sees No 1 *The Earl* and No 2 *Countess* climb towards Coppice Lane crossing.

1902 *(below)* – A night photo session at the Welshpool & Llanfair Light Railway's September galas sees *Countess* pose with two of the line's three replica Pickering carriages, all of which were built by the Ffestiniog Railway in the 21st century.

1902 – Former Dinorwic Quarry Hunslet 0-4-0ST *Alice* returned to steam on the Bala Lake Railway in 2010 following overhaul. It had previously steamed on the Leighton Buzzard Railway in the 1990s.

1903 – *Jurassic* is a Peckett 0-6-0ST built for the Southam Limeworks internal system in Warwickshire. In 1961, it moved to the Lincolnshire Coast Light Railway near Cleethorpes, a 2ft gauge line that made history by becoming the first to be laid on a green field site by enthusiasts. Built in 1958, using equipment from Lincolnshire's Nocton Potato Estate railway, it carried its first passengers in 1960, providing public transport to and from the Humberston Fitties holiday camp. Problems with the local council landlord saw it closed in 1985, but it was rebuilt at a new site at Skegness Water Leisure Park 35 miles away and reopened on 3 May 2009.

1905 – Bagnall 2-4-0T *Polar Bear* was the second locomotive built for the Groudle Glen Railway, a short 2ft gauge tourist line on the Isle of Man which was opened in 1896, closed in 1962 and revived from 1983 onwards. After closure, *Polar Bear* eventually found its way to Amnerley Museum in Sussex where it remains part of the fleet, but has revisited the Isle of Man in recent years.

1906 – *Russell* is a Hunslet 2-6-2T built for the North Wales Narrow Gauge Railways, later part of the Welsh Highland Railway. After the original WHR closed, *Russell* went to Brymbo Ironworks railway in Oxfordshire, and then to Fayle's Tramway, a ball clay mine railway on the Isle of Purbeck in Dorset before being saved by the Birmingham Locomotive Club and moved to the Talyllyn Railway for display. Now owned by the Welsh Highland Heritage railway at Portmadog, it is considered the 'flagship' survivor of the Welsh Highland. It is pictured at Rhiw Goch on the adjoining Ffestiniog Railway during a visit in 1988.

1908 (below) **–** In 1969, paper mill operator Bowaters handed over its 2ft 6in gauge line at Sittingbourne in Kent to the Locomotive Club of Great Britain, to run it as a preserved line, the Sittingbourne & Kemsley Light Railway, but sold some of the steam engines to Whipsnade Zoo for a new line being built in the grounds there. This view from 2010 shows three Bowaters engines reunited at the zoo: 1908-built Kerr Stuart 0-4-2T *Excelsior* and 1920-built Kerr Stuart 0-6-2T *Superior* with visiting SKLR stalwart 1924-built Kerr Stuart 0-4-2ST *Melior* (centre).

1908 — *Graf Schwerin-Lowitz*, an 0-6-2 well tank built by Arn Jung of Germany which ran on the now-closed Mecklenburg-Pommersche Schmalspurbahn in the former East Germany. It is now part of the service fleet on the 1ft 11¾in gauge Brecon Mountain Railway, a tourist line opened in June 1980 on part of the trackbed of the standard gauge Brecon & Merthyr Railway route, which had been axed by British Railways in 1964.

1909 *(opposite)* — K1, the world's first articulated Garratt locomotive, hauls the Welsh Highland Railway's Pullman observation car through the Aberglaslyn Pass. Supplied new as one of a pair to Tasmania's North-East Dundas Tramway in 1909 by the Manchester firm of Beyer Peacock, they were placed in storage after the line closed in 1929.

Sold back to its manufacturer in 1947, by then the 0-4-0+0-4-0 had become an amalgamation of parts of both K1 and K2. It was then sold to the Ffestiniog Railway in 1966, although it was too tall and too wide for use on the line. As the Ffestiniog's plans for rebuilding the Welsh Highland progressed, K1 was seen as perfect motive power for the trans-Snowdon route, and so it was restored, moving under its own power at Boston Lodge Works for the first time on 22 August 2004.

1909, 1917 – The Apedale Valley Light Railway is a new 2ft gauge line and museum near Newcastle-under-Lyme established by the Moseley Railway Trust, which has one of the biggest collections of industrial narrow gauge stock in Britain. The aim is to run industrial loco-motives in a state as near as possible as they were built, rather than

their later modified form for heritage railway passenger working. Pictured left is 1909-built large Quarry Hunslet 0-4-ST *Edward Sholto*, repatriated from the USA in 2006 by enthusiast Andrew Neale, and the trust's Kerr Stuart Tattoo class 0-4-2ST *Stanhope*, which was sold to Holloway Brothers of Inverkeithing for use on construction of the naval dockyard at Rossyth before helping to build the Sidcup bypass in Kent. In 1930, Durham County Water Board used it on the Weardale Reservoir contract and here it it received its name, from a local village. In 1934 it ended up at Penrthyn Quarry and worked until 1948, finally being preserved in 1966 after many of its components went missing.

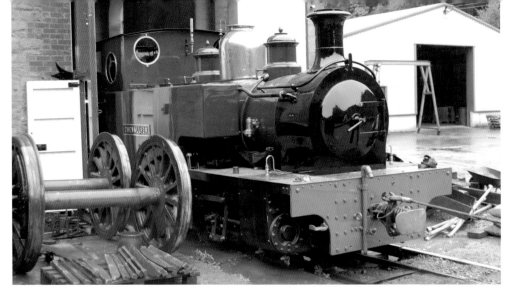

1915 – Manning Wardle 0-6-2T *Chevalier* was supplied to the Royal Navy's 2ft gauge Chattenden & Upnor Railway at Chatham, and in 1950 sold to the nearby Bowaters paper mill railway, the last steam-operated industrial narrow gauge railway in Britain. In 1969 it was sold to Whipsnade Zoo, and in 2010 current owner Bill Parker restored it. *Chevalier* is seen emerging from Bill's Flour Mill Colliery workshop at Bream in the Forest of Dean.

1915 – A Kerr Stuart "Joffre" class 0-6-0T was bought by Lynton & Barnstaple Railway revivalists in 1983, and named *Axe*, after the original line's policy of calling its engines after three-letter Devon rivers. Finally, restored to working order in 2008, *Axe* now works most passenger trains at Woody Bay.

1917 – The Baldwin 10-12-DS were a class of 1 ft 11⅝in 4-6-0 pannier talks built in the USA for the British War Department Light Railways for service in France, Egypt and Palestine during the First World War. After the war, several were sold to British narrow gauge lines including the Glyn Valley Tramway, Ashover Light Railway, Welsh Highland Railway and Snailbeach District Railways. Two are preserved: No 778 was restored to working order at the Leighton Buzzard Railway while No 598 is at the Welsh Highland Heritage Railway.

1918 – This Barclay 0-4-0 well tank was supplied new to the Airservice Construction Corps and from 1921 until 1945 it worked at the 2ft gauge RAF railway at Calshot Spit, Southampton. It was bought in 1949 by Abelson & Co. (Engineers) Ltd. The company presented it to the Talyllyn Railway in 1953. It was regauged to 2ft 3in gauge and renamed *Douglas* at the request of the donor. It entered service in 1954 and is pictured in 1995, with a new boiler and repainted in its old Air Ministry Works & Buildings colours. It is now painted red and running as Thomas & Friends character *Duncan*.

1918, 1922 *(opposite)* — The Kerr Stuart Wren class 0-4-0STs were amongst the smallest 2ft gauge loco-motives built, and were popular as contractors' engines and for use at smaller industrial sites. Three came together at the Devon Railway Centre, which has a 2ft gauge running line laid from Cadeleigh Station on the Great Western Railway's Exe Valley line. They are, left to right, Leighton Buzzard Railway-based *Pixie* (built 1922), No 3114 of 1918, on loan from the Vale of Rheidol Railway, and *Peter Pan* (built 1922), also from Leighton Buzzard.

1918, 1948, 1957 *(below)* — The South Tynedale Railway is a 2ft gauge tourist line laid on the southern-most part of the trackbed standard gauge Alston branch in Cumbria, and which uses steam engines imported from the continent. Pictured are 1957-built Polish 0-6-0 tender locomotive *Naklo* (centre), and Henschel 0-4-0Ts *Helen Kathryn*, built 1948 (far right) and *Thomas Edmondson*, built 1918.

PIXIE

Passengers
must not cross
the line

1919 *(opposite)* – In 1962, enthusiast vicar the Reverend Teddy Boston bought Bagnall 0-4-0ST *Pixie* from Cranford ironstone quarry near Kettering and used it as the basis for a 2ft gauge running line in the garden of his rectory at Cadeby in Leicestershire. After he died in 1986, his widow Audrey kept the unique railway open until 2005, holding regular open days. *Pixie* was sold and moved to the Hollycombe Steam Collection near Liphook, Hampshire.

1921 *(below)* – This Kerr Stuart 0-4-2ST became No 4 in the Corris Railway fleet when supplied new. The line was closed in 1948, the first year of British Railways ownership, and three years later, it and No 3, the other surviving locomotive on the defunct line, were bought by the newly-formed Talyllyn

Railway Preservation Society, which needed more stock for the rare 2ft 3in gauge shared by both lines. The pair retained their number in the Talyllyn fleet, No 3 being named *Sir Haydn* and No 4 *Edward Thomas*.

1923 – After the Great Western Railway inherited the 1ft 11¾in Vale of Rheidol Railway, which had opened in 1902, it replaced the original locomotives with similar models. Two new 2-6-2Ts were built at Swindon in 1923: the new No 7 and No 8 were named *Owain Glyndwr* and *Llywellyn* respectively in 1926. No 7 is seen heading towards the Devils' Bridge terminus.

1923 – Vale of Rheidol Railway No 8 *Llewellyn*, built to a similar design to the Aberystwyth-Devil's Bridge line's original Davies & Metcalf 2-6-2Ts, none of which survive.

1923 – Although a public passenger-carrying line seven miles long, the Lake District's 15in gauge Ravenglass & Eskdale Railway's locomotives have more in common with seaside miniature railways, in that they appear to be scaled-down versions of standard gauge types. *River Esk*, a 2-8-2, was supplied by Davey Paxman in 1923.

1924 – The two new GWR 2-6-2Ts for the Vale of Rheidol Railway were followed in 1924 by a 'refurbished' No 2 *Prince of Wales*, which was in effect a new locomotive built from a third set of parts, described as a 'heavy overhaul' just to satisfy the Swindon accountants, whereas the original Davies & Metcalf No 2 had been scrapped. It later became No 9 in the fleet.

1924 – While steam haulage on the British Rail main line ended on 11 August 1968, a tiny part of the BR empire continued to use steam on passenger trains. The London Midland Region saw the popularity of preserved lines like the Ffestiniog and the Talyllyn and decided to keep the Vale of Rheidol Railway. However, adhering to BR's dogmatic 'one size fits all' policy, the three engines and carriages had to carry the corporate blue livery introduced in 1964, complete with double arrow logos, and were even designated as Class 98, in line with the diesel and electric traction numbering system. No 9 *Prince of Wales* is seen in BR blue livery. In April 1989, the railway was sold to the owners of the Brecon Mountain Railway.

1925 – Following in the same vein as the Ravenglass & Eskdale Railway, the Romney, Hythe & Dymchurch is akin to a 'main line in miniature' with scaled-down standard gauge types on 15 gauge track. Here, No 1 *Green Goddess*, built by Davey Paxman, heads towards Dungeness in July 2009.

1930 – Baldwin 4-6-2 No 2 is one of the biggest steam locomotives ever to run on a British narrow gauge line, in this case the Brecon Mountain Railway. Built in Philadelphia, No 2 spent its working life hauling limestone near Port Elizabeth in  South Africa. In 1974 it ran away with its train minus its driver and crashed a few miles down the line. An insurance write-off, it was sold for scrap value, shipped to Liverpool and completely rebuilt in the line's workshops at Pant.

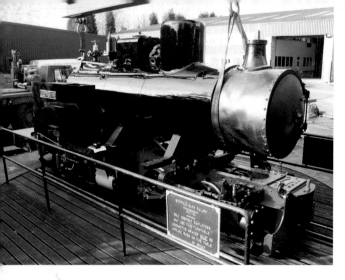

1930 – Swiss engineer Anatole Mallet's articulated locomotives found favour all round the globe, apart from Britain. In 2011, this Jung-built 0-4-4-0T, No 4878, one of several locomotives bought from Indonesian sugar plantation lines by Graham Lee, owner of Hunslet-Barclay, was unveiled at his private Statfold Barn Railway near Tamworth, and later visited the Welsh Highland Railway. There, it became the first Mallet to haul public passenger trains in Britain.

1936, 1958 *(opposite)* **–** Today's rebuilt Welsh Highland Railway uses articulated Garratt locomotives as the mainstay of its steam fleet. The Garratt concept was perfectly suited to difficult terrain in third world countries, and these 2-6-2+2-6-2 locomotives were supplied to South African Railways where they became Class NGG16 on the 2ft gauge system. A pair is seen arriving at the temporary terminus of Hafod y Llyn with the VIP Aberglaslyn Pas Opening Train on 21 May 2009. In front is No 87, built by Cockerill of Belgium in 1936, backed by No 143, built by Beyer Peacock in Manchester in 1958.

1936/1958 – At first the Welsh Highland Garratts seem like giants compared to 'ordinary' narrow gauge locomotives, as if they were standard gauge engines built to 2ft gauge. Yet in the mountains of Snowdonia, they are dwarfed by the landscape. Nos 87 and 143 are seen returning to Caernarfon.

1944 *(below)* – This 2ft gauge Peckett 0-6-0ST was built for the Harrogate Gas Works. It was sold in 1956 to the Ffestiniog Railway, but was unsuitable for the line's tight clearances. Eventually it found its way to the Statfold Barn Railway where it was fully restored.

1946 – Cut-down Barclay 0-4-0T Dougal was built for service amidst the tight clearances of Provan Gasworks in Glasgow. Too small for passenger working at its Welshpool & Llanfair Light Railway home, it nonetheless features in special events.

1949, 1991 – This 0-4-2T is a new locomotive 'by the back door'. *Tom Rolt*, named after the founder of the Talyllyn Railway Preservation Society, was built at the line's Pendre Works, incorporating components of a little-used 3ft gauge Andrew Barclay 0-4-0WT built in 1949 for Bord na Mona (the Irish Turf Board) nicknamed *Irish Pete*. The railway's newest, and most powerful steam locomotive, it entered service in 1991.

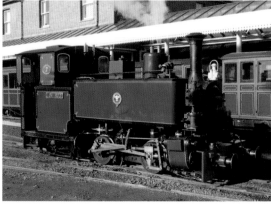

1971 – Popular myth has it that British Railways Standard 9F 2-10-0 No 92220 *Evening Star* was the last steam engine built for commercial purposes in the UK. However, the honour goes to Hunslet 0-4-2ST *Trangkil* No 4 (works number 3902 of 1971), built at Leeds for service on a sugar plantation in Indonesia, and repatriated in 2004 by Hunslet Engine Company owner Graham Lee for use on his Statfold Barn Railway, where it made its debut in 2005 after being regauged from 2ft 6in to 2ft.

1979 – A landmark on the preserved Ffestiniog Railway came in 1979 when, 110 years after *Little Wonder* appeared on the line, a brand new double Fairlie, *Earl of Merioneth*, based on the original patent, although with modern box-like side tanks, emerged from Boston Lodge Works.

1982 – The Ffestiniog Railway broke more ground in 1982 with the building of a second heritage era double Fairlie, 0-4-0+0-4-0T *David Lloyd George*, at Boston Lodge Works.

1986 – The Romney, Hythe & Dymchurch Railway long claimed to be the world's smallest public railway, but lost the crown in 1982 to the Wells & Walsingham Light Railway which was laid by retired naval commander Roy Francis over part of the Great Eastern Railway's Wells-next-the-Sea branch to 10¼in gauge, a size otherwise associated with miniature railways. In 1986, a 2-6-0 + 0-6-2 articulated Garratt, *Norfolk Hero*, named after Admiral Lord Nelson was built, followed by a second, *Norfolk Heroine*, in 2010.

2005 – Enthusiast groups who build new steam engines from scratch often do so to recreate an extinct type of locomotive. In the case of the Corris Railway Society, which could not buy back the line's surviving No 4 from the Talyllyn Railway, this was not the case. Instead, it was decided to build a new locomotive based on No 4's Kerr Stuart Tattoo class design, and so Corris 0-4-2ST No 7 was produced.

2006 – Graham Lee, owner of Hunslet-Barclay, who has been developing his own multiple-gauge private Statford Barn Railway near Tamworth, established the Hunslet Engine Company to build new steam locomotives in the twenty-first century, based on traditional designs. The first was a new Quarry Hunslet 0-4-0ST named *Statfold*, and was followed by a cabless version with a taller chimney, *Jack Lane*, named after the address of the original Hunslet works in Leeds.

They were allocated works numbers 3903 and 3904 respectively, continuing the historic Hunslet steam locomotive numbering series, and have visited many heritage lines.

2010 – Four of the five original Lynton & Barnstaple Railway locomotives were scrapped after the legendary 1ft 11½in gauge line in North Devon closed in 1935. The fifth, *Lew*, was exported to South America, but despite international efforts by enthusiasts, nobody has been able to establish its fate. However, in September 2010, a replica Manning Wardle 2-6-2T closely based on *Lew*, named *Lyd*, and built at the Ffestiniog Railway's Boston Lodge workshops over a 15-year period, appeared on the revived L&B at Woody Bay in black, hauling an original L&B coach borrowed from the FR, along with the latter's first-class observation saloon, based on a L&B design.

2010 – During December 2010, the Ffestiniog Railway decided to repaint *Lyd* into mock British Railways livery – which the Southern Railway-built engine would almost certainly have carried had the Lynton & Barnstaple Railway survived into nationalisation. No 30190 is the next available number after No 188 *Lew* and 72E was the shedcode for Barnstaple's outlying sheds.

2011 *(opposite)* – Then it its final stages of building, *Lyd* carried lined Southern Railway green livery for public display in early 2010. This is the permanent livery it will carry, just like its predecessor *Lew*.

Acknowledgements

Grateful thanks for the following photographs:

Cover Phil Brown/FR Co; 28 centre, 30, 31, 32, 33, 34, 37, 40, 41,43 (all),44, 45, 46 top, 59, 60, 61 Paul Jarman, Beamish Museum; 2, 55, 57 Isle of Man Tourism; 5, 58 Swansea Museum; 11, 13, 17, 20 (both) London Transport Museum; 22 Middleton Railway; 29 (both) Crich Tramway Village; 35 top Mark S Jobling; 36, 37 Brian Lindop, Blackpool Tramways; 47, 48 Black Country Living Museum; 50, 51, 52, 53 Seaton Tramway; 54 Colin Paxton/Great Orme Tramway; 62 Tim Green/Creative Commons; 63 Transport for London; 64 Granada TV.